Stripped

A Collection of Poems Written in Recovery

Cissy Stag

Dedication

I'd like to dedicate this book to every person who chose not to see me or hear me when I roared. My value is not contingent on your approval. I wrote this book despite your attempts to strip me of my humanity. I love you. I hate you. I'm indifferent to you. Thank you for showing me the importance of loving myself.

Stripped

Introduction

Hi. I'm Cissy. I started a business making glitter heels for strippers and pole dancers in July 2023. I failed epically during my first year of business. My content struck a nerve with my new community in North Carolina. I was intensely cyberbullied and ostracized. By August 18, 2023, I had my first stalker on Instagram.

Triggered by stress from being cyberbullied and stalked by a collective, I experienced my first psychotic episode. I developed intense surveillance delusions while in psychosis. You know how some people pray to God? I prayed to the Federal Bureau of Investigation.

On February 20, 2024, the day after my 31st birthday, I was incarcerated for contempt of court in Raleigh, North Carolina. I'd been freshly diagnosed with Autism, Borderline Personality Disorder, and Post-Traumatic Stress Disorder a month prior.

After I was released from jail, I was desperate for an outlet to express myself. Instagram had become an unsafe and volatile space for me to tell my story. I stopped talking about my life experiences and started writing poetry.

Poetry carried me through intense episodes of fear, depression, and through the development of suicidal ideations. Every bit of what I knew about my identity had been Stripped. Poetry allowed me to reclaim my voice.

Stripped is my collection of poems that explore unhealthy attachment, queerness, fantasy, friendship, betrayal, religion, spirituality, love, hate, hurt, healing, power, and the impact of social media on one's psyche. Stripped is a creative piece inspired by my life experiences. It is not a factual retelling of events.

Table of Contents

"The Enclosure"

I told you in the summer that my enclosure was made of glass.

In the fall, you became curious about my habitat.

So, you started knocking on the glass.

The glass began to crack, but I was still inside. Comfortable but a little bit annoyed by the noise.

By winter, you recruited the other guests. People who also were peeking through my enclosure and wanted to get inside.

Forty fists banging on the glass until it finally broke.

And you SHRIEKED because the shards hurt your hands.

And I screamed and cried because you made a mess of my enclosure.

Pieces of glass everywhere. In the moss. In the vines. In the flowers.

So, I left. And when I left, I stepped in the glass.

My feet bleeding.

Afraid. Confused. And hallucinating from the pain.

The enclosure is yours now.

I'm outside.

I'm uncomfortable out here.

The tiny pieces of glass remain embedded in my feet.

When you entered the enclosure, you learned that it wasn't what you expected.

So, you followed me back out into the world. Still watching.

Screaming because you perceive me to be an animal.

But I'm the one you set free.

It is spring.

And while you may still hunt me,

I am alive.

"The Haunted House: Part 1"

Stuck.

In a haunted house.

In a place filled with ghosts of my delusions.

A fantasy that keeps me trapped.

Full.

Not with dreams.

But with nightmares.

Nightmares of monsters with long claws.

Telling me that I am unworthy.

That I do not deserve to be loved.

To be respected.

To be seen.

To be heard.

Monsters that scream at me to get out while clutching on to my wrists and ankles to ensure that I cannot leave.

I've been here so long that the monsters no longer scare me.

But they drain me.

I feel weak because I have been screaming and thrashing for so long.

I want nothing more than to touch base with reality.

Truth.

Not their version of what happened.

"The Haunted House: Part 2"

In The Haunted House,

And I see a window.

Can I run?

Can I climb?

Can I make it out in time?

I don't know.

But I'm going to try.

"The Haunted House: Part 2"

"The Haunted House: Part 3"

7 months.

That's how long I have been in The Haunted House.

I always sensed your presence but thought you to be a ghost.

You were screaming too.

Until, finally, you screamed in my face.

And I could see you.

Flesh and blood. And terrified like me.

The window is right there.

I'm making a run for it.

Because I want out.

I hope you decide to run too.

The world outside is big enough for us to part ways.

"The Haunted House: Part 4"

Awake from the rain.

Awake from the nightmare.

I'm standing outside The Haunted House with my face pressed against the window.

I know that the outside world is where I belong.

And yet, I stand here.

Ready to climb back into the chaos.

My feet sink into the mud as I ruminate.

And again, I feel stuck.

I HAVE to go this time.

Pull my heels from the earth before it swallows me.

And go.

"Escape from The Haunted House: Part 1"

Daylight breaks, and I am standing on the grounds of The Haunted House.

I feel blinded by the sun - my pupils small for so long.

My ears ringing.

Tinnitus from the screams.

My nostrils filled with the stench of the last few seasons.

Do I cover my eyes? My ears?

Do I hold my nose?

Frozen in my inability to decide.

And still sinking into the earth below me.

I dislodge my heel from the muck and step forward.

My stiletto sinks back.

In retrospect, I shouldn't have worn high heels to a haunted house.

But they are the only shoes I have.

And the yard is littered with glass.

Forward I go.

Slowly.

Carefully.

But forward, nonetheless.

"Escape from The Haunted House: Part 2"

Another step forward, and I am ready to remove my shoes.

Turn back.

I scan the perimeter.

There is glass everywhere.

If I take them off and run back, I risk laceration.

I risk bleeding out.

I risk infection.

My skin is red from the sun.

My muscles burn with lactic acid.

I feel my nerves come alive and then wither...

It hurts.

I hurt.

I'm angry.

I heard your confession as I climbed out of the window.

The part of me that found comfort in chaos is ready to sprint.

Dive back in through the window,

Feet bleeding.

And scream your confession right back into your face.

But then... that puts me right back in The Haunted House

Where inevitably, the demons will take over.

I remember when I thought I would die if I didn't know.

I was so afraid.

And now I know.

It just hurts.

So, I'm keeping the goddamn heels on.

My ankles blister.

I am taking another step.

Away from the house.

Away from the ghosts.

I'm not turning around this time.

Not to check if you are following me.

Not to watch for the Hellhounds.

They are still asleep.

My mind is still there...

But my body is OUT.

I'm going.

Step by step.

Turning back will not undo what is done.

It will not make what happened to me fair.

It will just drain me...

Until I become a ghost,

And I become trapped in the house for eternity.

I pull my heel from the muck once more.

I keep going.

My mind will catch up.

"Escape from The Haunted House: Part 3"

I almost turned back.

I almost ditched my shoes and RAN.

Through the shattered glass.

Right back through the window

And climbed inside The Haunted House.

Because I heard screaming.

And it hurt.

Every inch of my body.

Every nerve.

Burning alive.

With rage.

With desperation.

With heartbreak.

So, I almost turned back.

I almost climbed back in.

Because I thought if I went back

And I screamed right in your face,

It would be the only thing to make my pain go away.

And then I felt guilty.

I felt shame.

Because I know you are still in the house.

And then I wanted to run back to save you.

Help you out.

Give you a boost.

And hurt myself further by doing that.

And tell myself it was worth the pain.

It's not.

The screams were not yours this time.

They were mine.

Turning back will not make my pain go away.

So I pull my heel from the muck once again.

And I take another step forward.

Into the daylight without you.

Because your approval will not heal my wounds.

If you want out of The Haunted House, the window is right there.

You are strong enough to climb out.

This time, I'm not coming back.

"Early Spring"

The spring air feels like fall today as I touch projects that are months abandoned.

March.

I know that we are in March.

Only five months from August.

And it feels like I'm right back where I was in October.

Jaded.

Confused.

Wondering why I am still bothered.

And afraid it will never stop.

I find no value in being the bigger person.

I don't want to be bigger.

I just want to be a person at peace.

So, I inhale this spring air.

It smells like fall too.

And I open my eyes.

I scan the perimeter.

It is spring.

It is time to stop worrying about forever.

It is time to focus on now.

"Heart"

A heart this big may not be wicked.

It may be perceived as beautiful.

But a heart this big is inflamed.

It is indicative of disease.

But still it beats.

"Heart"

"Authenticity"

"Be your authentic self." AND "Don't let them know that you are bothered."

Okay, and how the... FUCK... am I supposed to do both when you are always watching?

A mask half on is still a mask.

And I am SWEATING under this bitch.

My pores are clogged.

My skin itches.

I want to rip it OFF.

So, what if my appearance beneath my mask disgusts you?

You were not satisfied when my mask was on.

No matter how I present, you do not look away.

"MySpace"

Release.

Release this idea of how I should or shouldn't be.

Release myself from worries of you watching.

And wondering if you are bothered.

You bothered ME.

You watched ME.

You tried to destroy ME.

And yeah.

I'm damaged now.

I'm in pain.

I don't trust easily.

But I'm still alive.

And maybe I don't feel like dancing tonight.

But I can stand here.

Inhale.

Exhale.

Ground myself.

And remind myself...

This is MY space.

Not yours.

"Labyrinth"

10 years.

That's how long I have walked the labyrinth of this place.

On sleepless nights like this.

And nights that I felt fulfilled.

I don't feel that way right now.

This place looks a lot different than it did 10 years ago...

Hell, it looks a lot different than it did 3 years ago.

As do I.

This place has improved.

But I loved it back when the water ran brown,

And the floors were warped.

They still kind of are...

This place stands strong.

Like me.

For a decade, it was my escape.

And now it is my home.

"Façade"

Two hours.

That's how long it takes you to build your new façade before you come knocking at my door.

You run away and hide in the yard.

You stand in the bushes and peep through the windows to see if I answer.

I remain seated.

I don't have to check the door to know that it is you.

I see you right there.

Face pressed against the glass.

Your glasses are new, but you kept the same fake mustache.

My door remains locked.

I get up, and I close the curtains.

"Triggered: Part 1"

Four days.

That's how long it has been since they last triggered you.

And for four days, you have struggled with compulsions...

And desires to tell them everything.

Why they hurt you.

Detail the damage that they did.

And why you still believe in them.

For four days, you wrote them.

And you didn't hit send.

Yesterday was different.

You wrote.

And you never addressed it to them.

You didn't finish the letter.

Because you realized that you were writing once again to the fantasy version of them.

Not to their true identity...

So, you tore the page from your journal.

You crumpled up the paper and tossed it in the bin with the others.

You struck a match and dropped it in.

And you watched the bin burn.

Slowly at first.

And then the contents went up in a blaze.

You wept for yourself.

And then you wrote this instead.

You wrote.

And you wrote.

And you wrote.

Mountains of words that you could be proud of.

While still acknowledging the pain.

Still acknowledging the shame.

And you know.

This is more rewarding.

"Art"

Create art.

That's the plan.

There is no backup.

My art wasn't always stupid.

But when you said it was, I believed you.

Because I hadn't recovered from the trauma of you.

From your split.

From the rapidness with which you built your wall of stones.

I wished you well as you stood on the other side - out of my sight.

You peered over at your leisure.

And spoke your dark magic onto me.

Wishing me unwell.

Here we are - 7 months later.

I caught you peering over your stone wall.

To Hell with your hex!

My art is not stupid.

It is magical.

I started a business, and you destroyed me for it.

Look me in my eyes and tell me that's not what happened.

"Escape from The Haunted House: Part 4"

On the grounds of The Haunted House, and I approach the gate.

It's unlocked.

I scan the perimeter.

The Hellhounds...

They are nowhere to be found.

Are they still sleeping?

Or are they simply ignoring your whistles?

It does not matter.

The gate is RIGHT THERE.

It is UNLOCKED.

So, I open it.

I pull my heel from the muck.

And I take my first step out.

Out of bounds.

From the perimeter.

And away from The Haunted House.

"Our Lips Are Sealed"

I started a business,

And you destroyed me for it.

When it was yours, it was art.

When it was mine, it was stupid.

When you showed others your suffering, you were vulnerable.

When I showed others my suffering, I was Batshit.

...

Your secrets were unearthed.

Not because you shared them.

Because I worked hard.

I learned.

I echoed your secrets back to you,

And I told you mine.

Your secrets are mine now.

I'm keeping my lips sealed.

Triple sealed.

"Conversations with Iffy"

I gaze out the window while seated with my physician.

Sunlight fills the room.

"How are you doing?" she asks.

And I answer honestly.

I have been better.

This is what happened.

I have been experiencing so many triggers.

So, I'm anxious.

And I just feel sad.

I detail my experience for my physician.

And I ask, "Will increasing my medications help with the sadness?"

She tells me, "Anyone in your position would be stressed. I don't want to increase your medications to the point that you become loopy. Keep talking to your therapist. I'm here for you."

Validation.

Reassurance.

The little things that make a big difference.

I'm on the right path this time. Even though it's bumpy.

For the first time, I do not cry while talking to my physician.

We laugh over the stench of bologna and cornflakes at 4:30 in the morning.

"I'm not made for this place," I say.

She howls with laughter. "That's someone's diamond."

"Eggshells"

Yesterday.

I paced the garden and found my words.

My words of blades.

My words of venom.

A commentary.

On the false love you seek from society.

I thought them, but I couldn't write them.

I went home.

I crawled in bed.

At the garden, I wrote these words.

I remembered that I wished you well.

And you wished me dead.

So, I thought my words of wrath.

And I wrote down these instead.

Eggshells.

I take another step forward and hear them crunching below my feet.

My mind paces backwards.

I remember exactly how I felt in that moment.

Like I was walking on eggshells

Trying not to make a noise.

"Darkness"

I thought I knew darkness.

And then I met you.

I examine the details of the fallout.

The hatred in your words.

And your hurt that you chose to inflict on me.

The way that you preyed on my insecurities,

And then told me I was not worthy of your pity.

I couldn't believe my eyes.

I couldn't believe my ears.

I couldn't believe my mind.

Your void is incomparable.

And it's not my responsibility.

I cannot save you.

And I cannot save the others from your darkness.

You hide it well.

But now that I know.

I'm diving headfirst.

Into the silver lining between the storm clouds.

And I am finding my light.

I choose to save ME.

"Exit"

I missed my exit.

I saw it too late.

The other cars wouldn't let me over.

So, I kept driving.

I took the long way.

I rerouted.

The long route is the route that I choose.

Speeding towards my exit risks collision.

And I don't know if it would hurt other people.

But it would hurt me.

So, it's not worth it.

I missed my exit, and the scenery wasn't pretty.

But it gave me this profound thought.

Inspiration grew from the mundane.

So, I wrote about it.

And I shared it.

"War"

The war in my mind continues.

I begged for peace from you.

And now I finally have it.

But I haven't found peace myself.

I lie here and come to realizations...

Of the things that you did that I did not think possible.

It all makes sense.

Finally.

And then I worry.

I have this moment of peace.

A blip of Heaven in the constant Hell that I faced.

How much longer until my Earth is shattered again?

I want this life.

I want this peace to be more than a glitch in my reality.

The sun is warm.

The air is comfortable.

And my mind is still battling demons.

I feel like I'm not able to enjoy this moment.

Because I fear that I may never truly know peace.

"Breathe"

I no longer feel your presence, and I can finally breathe.

"Freckles"

Freckles.

I don't think about them much.

But you talk about them plenty.

"Two Sides"

I pace the streets of an oil-slicked town.

All the colors swirling in puddles.

Beneath the surface lies a dime in the rubble.

Two sides to every coin.

I ponder the saying, and I see Blue.

The Blue of the ocean water that flooded my ears.

And blinded my eyes, burning with salt.

I remember having my flame extinguished as I sunk to the depths of the unknown.

I wasn't in town when it happened.

You burned bright - flames of blood red.

The others admired your hue.

They burned orange.

"Pour kerosene on the streets," you told them.

"It will make your flame burn red like mine."

So, the orange flames did.

The town caught fire.

A blaze so hot that it burned Blue.

It burned Blue for you.

When the rain came, the fire was extinguished.

And it brought me.

The town is gray.

Gray shells of the houses that once stood bright.

Creeks of rainbow flow through the cracks in the asphalt.

How strange is it that only a dime survived the fire?

Two sides to every coin.

I consider reaching down to pick it up.

To examine it carefully.

Just to be SURE.

But then I don't.

I already know that there are two sides.

"Connections"

The air is getting warmer.

I flip through the gallery of my Nikon...

And watch the movie of my old life play.

Special moments.

With people who were special to me then.

How far and distant we became as the seasons changed...

We grew up and grew apart,

From the stages of our lives already separated by time.

I miss those moments.

But I cannot forget the moments that followed.

The isolation.

The screaming.

The power struggle...

Not everyone deserves forgiveness.

The movie is bliss.

Ignorance.

Novelty.

And ultimately a reminder of lost connections.

Connections built with shorts in the wiring.

What's the worst that could happen?

"Blood"

Poetry doesn't always cut it.

For now,

I'll bite my lip

And expect it to bleed.

"Hunted"

The Hellhounds caught up to me in the town.

Their orange red eyes glowed in the abyss of night.

I crouched low, taking cover beneath the gray husk of a home that once stood bright pink.

My eyes still sting from the ocean's depth.

My hair is stiff with salt, and I know that I am protected.

Daylight breaks, but I do not.

"Smog"

The smog of morning has cleared.

I'm face to face with you,

And for the first time,

I don't see you with my heart.

I see you with my eyes.

I pause.

I inhale.

The air reeks.

It's you.

I exhale.

"Ignorance"

I watch this film back and listen to the words spoken.

The hope.

The excitement.

And I laugh.

A moment out of my control that led to so much disappointment.

But a disappointment that brought me to this place instead.

My naive soul sent me to Hell and back.

I feel the sun on my skin today.

The wind blows - cooling the heat of Georgia.

Inhale.

Exhale.

Back.

I made it back.

"Privacy"

I wrote down my experiences.

My frustrations.

I almost posted them.

And then I saved them to my "notes" app instead.

I owe myself the privacy that you did not have the grace to give me.

"Verdict"

Innocent.

A funny way to describe those who do not know that they did not earn your trust when you called them that.

Do you intend to tell them that I'm your favorite?

Or do you expect me to keep your secret after you told all of mine?

"Hypocrisy"

Vile.

A funny way to describe a mind that you seek like a drug.

A body and soul that carries trauma that you did not understand as you inflicted more.

Stories that you try to claim as your own in the name of altruism.

Your elitism blinds your judgment.

Your entitlement cracks the foundation of your narrative.

None of it is yours.

It is mine.

"Garner"

The wind blows.

I am seated in the spot that I sat many times before.

Where I shared good experiences.

And bad experiences.

About my life.

About my mental health.

I remember November 2022.

When I knew that this place was "the one".

But I'd yet to meet the people here.

I remember becoming so scared of this place when the demons invited themselves in.

I never thought it would be a safe haven for me after the trauma... but then it was.

Instagram isn't real life.

I remind myself of that often.

Although it sure as shit feels like it can be at times.

It is not.

And so I remind myself...

I may have come to this place as authentically as I could...

But others didn't.

And that's not my problem.

"Florida"

Sometimes, I wish that I'd never left Tallahassee.

But then I replay the things that were said about me after I left.

When people crumpled up a decade of relationships for someone more sparkly.

And I wonder... is that how you felt about me all along?

Through the performances.

The holidays.

The moments in life that were special to me.

Were they not special to you too?

And I think about that someone more sparkly.

Someone who would not have been valued in the way that they were if not for the way that I sung their praises.

And how during all of this...

They wanted me.

Alive.

Dead.

Doesn't matter.

They wanted ME.

And it was flattering...

But flattery doesn't pay the bills.

So, know this.

While you pursue them...

They pursue me.

And it's not love.

It's mental illness.

Trust me.

I've been there.

And knowing then what I know now would have saved me a Hell of a lot of heartache.

Money.

And time.

Consider yourself lucky to not know what it is like to walk in my Pleasers.

"Return to The Haunted House"

I'm back in The Haunted House.

I'm not sure how I got here.

Did the Hellhounds find me?

Did I sleepwalk?

I'm seated.

Numb.

It's movie night.

I gaze forward.

Tears fill my eyes.

A hairy little monster extends its index finger towards the screen.

Then reaches back and clutches onto my thigh.

"You're a star."

I open my mouth to scream.

Nothing comes out.

"Foam"

Pins and needles in my body.

Eggshells below my feet.

I know that your goal wasn't to educate.

I know because I know you.

I know your army of performative artists.

And you know me.

I see you foaming at the mouth.

When I said what I said, I meant it.

Make the call.

"Forgive Me"

I wished you well,

And you wished me dead.

Forgive me,

For I'm done forgiving you for the words that you said.

"Long Distance"

I live two lives.

One in the city.

And one with you.

My time split

But not wasted.

I never do long-distance,

But you are the exception to my rule.

"Long Distance"

"You"

Nights like this...

I remember them well.

I used to write her and feel so safe.

But she betrayed my trust...

And for what?

Praise from people unimportant to her?

Tonight, I write my dad.

I don't weep yet.

My expectations are low.

When I needed him most, he was gone.

The psychosis was not my fault.

But I got my own car towed anyway.

Without support.

Without understanding.

I hung up when the screaming began.

I only know three phone numbers.

And when I was incarcerated, I only dialed two.

My mom...

And you.

"Empathy"

"I have no empathy for people who use their mental illness as a crutch."

This grandiose statement makes my roll my eyes.

My mental illness isn't my mobility aid.

It's the reason that I'm limping.

And frankly, you were never due an explanation of why I couldn't walk on both feet.

I marked myself fragile and hoped that you'd handle me with care.

And then you shook me.

Excuse me if I have no sympathy for you for cutting your hands on the shattered pieces of me.

"I have no empathy."

You could have finished your statement there.

"Voicemail"

You didn't respond.

I should have been sad about it.

But I felt relief.

Last night, I was ready to forgive you for screaming at me when I was at my lowest.

And today I'm glad that you didn't give me the opportunity.

"Solicitations"

One piece of mail.

That's all it took to waste my Saturday.

At first, I laughed.

And thought, "God, I hate you."

But the laughter subsided when I returned home.

Just to check my phone

And verify that you had not returned.

I don't want you back.

I want me back.

Me before you took everyone around me.

I don't want them back either.

Me before you toyed with my mind.

My life.

I'm taking those things back.

They were never yours to take.

I sit in bed and feel shame...

Because after all these months,

I'm still not okay.

"Court"

I'm most afraid that I will never get my answers.

Not of how I will feel if the answers are different from what I thought.

The court of public opinion is only free to those with no stake in the matter.

And frankly...

At this point...

I don't know who did what.

But I know why.

And the why is why you are no longer allowed in my life.

Any of you.

"Old Flames"

"You are not supposed to end up with your twin flame."

I heard that,

And I knew...

I knew from the day that I laid eyes on what you created.

Long before I saw you.

Long before I met you.

Draw from your deck.

Lovers are not as they appear.

Twin flames.

Two sides to a coin.

You and me.

We don't end up together.

"Actions"

So, we don't think in words...

You think in numbers,

And I think in actions.

Believe me, babe, you have the numbers.

But I know that your numbers only offer words.

They offer no actions.

And they only flocked to you for your satisfaction...

Because of your attraction.

Keep them.

I don't think in numbers or words.

I think in actions.

And it's way too late for their retractions.

"Theft"

Stealing.

I'm so glad that I do not feel that in my feelings.

Their own words.

Who they are as beings.

I see them in a moment so freeing.

And maybe I'm a little bit narcissistic for giving myself credit.

But honestly if it keeps them alive...

If it makes them happy...

I'm glad that they said it.

If I'm a Mirrorball,

And they are the reflection,

Then I am happy to see them

Facing me in the opposite direction.

Stealing.

That's not what this is.

It's a moment of inspiration...

That makes me grateful to exist.

"Studio"

My space now is barely any bigger than the first dormitory where I lived alone.

Summer 2011.

One season before I met you.

It's a lot more expensive.

And this time, it's in the right city.

The city that called to me for a decade.

I was always supposed to be here.

But you were supposed to be here with me.

I remember summer 2014.

You came with me.

We drove for 5 hours in the storm.

And settled at this place in the dark of the night.

We cuddled on the third floor and watched Forensic Files.

Front of the building.

The water ran brown.

I'll never forget.

Because I live here now.

Back of the building.

Call me a romantic.

I picked this place because it makes me feel safe.

Just like you.

And it doesn't hurt to pass by our old room every day.

The story isn't over.

I'm just anxious because I want you with me.

"Endorsement"

The day that you valued your reputation over a human life, it was over for us.

That goes for all of you.

I know exactly what she did.

I know exactly why I am angry.

And many of you pretended to not be involved.

Meanwhile, you actively supported her.

You invaded my privacy to prove yourself to her.

I'm angry with her.

But I am angrier with you.

Because you love bombed me.

You friendship bombed me.

You earned my trust.

And when you saw me suffer, you let it happen.

And when I didn't recover on your timeline, you took her side.

Vile.

She called me that.

And now I call you that.

Because how could you witness so much destruction and choose to stay silent?

Or choose to actively contribute?

The court of public opinion is only free to those without a stake in the matter.

And I don't reimburse for your bad investments.

You give a new meaning to paying for your friends.

I hope it was worth it.

I'd rather be alone and be myself than mask for a mob of people who do not know themselves.

Honestly.

If you seek endorsement, move along.

And if you seek sponsorship, go to Hell.

"Little"

Two hours.

I only slept two hours before I woke with a stomach full of fire.

Anxiety that I'd said too much in my own damn space.

One piece of mail.

That's how little a trigger can be to torture my mind.

And that's why none of them are allowed back in my life.

"31"

6 months ago.

I feel so much older now.

Less naive, but unsure that I am any wiser.

I remember the joy in this performance...

And how my image was used to torture me after.

Happy memories tarnished by the Hell that you put me through.

Everybody in this community... gone.

And I'd love to blame you for being a master manipulator...

But honestly... that community witnessed just a sliver of the Hell that you put me through and decided that it was okay.

So, I'll never forgive you.

And I'll never forgive them.

Thirty, flirty, and thriving.

That's all I wanted to be.

Look at me now... 31 and jaded.

"Depression: Part 1"

Countless hours of my life

I spend staring out this window.

Starving myself.

Feeling my muscles wasting away.

Grieving.

And wondering when I will run out of things and people to grieve.

My stomach burns.

I feel the chilly air grazing the surface of my skin.

It's time to get up.

The window is right there.

I can always return to this spot.

"Reach"

The numbers are in, and they are out of balance.

I know what this is.

I became DAMN good at pattern recognition.

I don't aim to please.

I aim to speak.

Eyes of vitriol remain fixated on me.

Mouths spilling over with foam.

I see the way that they burn with desire.

The way that they hope I will speak your name.

I'll keep them waiting forever.

This is me going with grace.

"Catfish"

Welcome back.

You were busy while I was sleeping.

I sip my midnight coffee and gaze forward.

It will never end, will it?

The windows are open.

The spring air smells like fall.

I cannot shake this feeling of familiarity.

Inhale.

Exhale.

I'm going to be okay.

"Intruder"

Gone already?

I'm sorry.

Did my hypervigilance scare you?

What a shame that I wasted your evening after you worked so hard on your new mask.

It was very pretty, though.

Three hours have passed.

I'm not having nightmares tonight.

A new dream was born of your visit.

It must exhaust you to be so inspiring.

"Blue"

I regret everything.

My heart burned Blue for your humanity.

To see you.

To hear you.

To reach you.

My heart burned in the winter to keep you warm,

And I lost my mind in the blaze.

Spirits fueled the flame, and the heat spread to my stomach.

And then it kept going.

Igniting every nerve ending like my body was made of paper.

I combusted.

Spring brought the rain.

March showers cooled the surface of my skin

And extinguished the inferno of your wrath.

I crumbled.

All that remains of me is ash.

"23"

I hate you.

There. I said it.

I jotted down my reasons,

And I stashed them away for safekeeping.

23.

There are 23 reasons that I hate you.

I'm biting my lip.

It's still bleeding.

"I Hate You"

There. I said it.

I hate you for asserting your ownership over my voice.

I hate you for taking my communities – new and old.

I hate you for never giving me peace.

I hate you for your manipulation.

I hate you for your false altruism.

I hate you for the triggers.

I hate you for my newfound enemies.

I hate you for exploiting me.

I hate you for scaring me.

I hate you for lying about my heart and mind.

I hate you for the institutionalization.

I hate you for the incarceration.

I hate you for filming me.

I hate you for publishing it.

I hate you for monitoring me.

I hate you for stalking me.

I hate you for the people sent to me who lied through their teeth to maintain access to me.

I hate you for letting me believe the craziest shit.

I hate you for accusing me of ruining your life while you set my life ablaze.

I hate you for laughing at me.

I hate you for prompting others to do the same.

I hate you for stonewalling me while my name still flooded your mouth.

I open my car door to unload my groceries, and I cannot move a muscle.

I hate you for that too.

"Fuck Me?"

No, thank you.

I know you'd like to.

But I'm busy.

Fucking myself...

While I think about how much I hate you.

"Code Switch"

A dozen plus whispers for seven months.

I never heard the voices.

But I can count.

So strange.

I don't remember registering for this affair.

Or this one.

Or that one.

The gag is in my mouth.

This happened to me.

Because of you.

And them.

Is it safe for me to come out?

No.

I write another line and think...

What's another color?

Another smell?

Another taste?

Another sensation?

Another way to describe the pain of my silent screams?

"Code Switch"

"The Industry"

Empowerment.

Ha!

The industry loves this word.

Buy THIS to feel EMPOWERED!

Move THIS way to feel EMPOWERED!

What if I can't move?

What if I freeze while in this space?

ANYONE can do it!

Anyone?

I can't.

Not anymore.

It took me ages to climb.

And even longer to invert.

My brain was always my biggest barrier.

The industry turned its back on me.

Do I really want to engage with those who only value diversity that is aesthetically pleasing?

The industry is ableist.

I called it out.

The industry responded...

YOU'RE JUST WEAK.

A LUNATIC.

The industry sent armed men to my door.

The industry said that I was a danger to the community.

I'm jaded by the industry.

Because the industry took my power.

"Revamp: Part 1"

The rain came, and this time, it wasn't a metaphor.

My days of sunshine were wasted in bed.

I'm not sure that you can call it rest if it makes you feel guilty.

The rain came and forced me to stay inside.

So, I pick my preoccupation for the day.

I scan the perimeter.

A desk.

A staging area.

Glitter.

Various glues.

And stacks upon stacks of platform heels.

Today, I return to my roots.

Forget the inspiration.

I started a business, and I did it by myself.

"Project"

I remember when I first made these heels.

I was so proud.

And then I got creative.

TOO creative.

It took me about an hour to scrape the gobs of Mod Podge.

And then the project rested.

For almost three months.

Is rest really an accurate word?

Neglect.

The project was neglected.

I was busy fighting demons.

Fighting for my life.

Fighting for my reputation.

Fighting for my story.

A story that the demons tried to claim as their own.

A story that the demons wish that they could tell and end with my demise.

I'm not dead.

And I hope that one day, my demons grow bored of me.

What can I say?

I must be a pleasure to watch.

"Senses"

I remember me before I was crazy.

Clinically speaking.

I remember when I was vulnerable.

Naive.

Full of hope.

The delusions eventually faded.

Reason stepped into the picture.

I scanned the perimeter and saw the damage that was done.

And remembered how I was the best source of information for the arsonist.

The fire has long been extinguished, but the scent of smoke lingers.

Will I ever clear my senses?

"Happy"

The sun begins to rise.

I analyze my list of what ifs from last night.

What if you never speak to me again?

And that's the thing that makes me happy.

"Fawns and Vices"

What if I stop begging people who walked away to reconnect?

What if I remember that when I asked for help, they declined?

What if my relationship with my vice has changed?

What if it's traumatizing me further?

What if I decide to get better?

What if I start taking a chance on myself the way that I wish others took a chance on me?

What if today I just cry?

And watch TV.

And rest.

"Snowfall"

I wrote a poem to gather my thoughts...

And realized how few memories I have from the first six months.

I wade through my gallery and spot the reasons for my spotty memory.

Good news.

Followed by bad news.

Some people.

Some I loved then...

But will not again.

Some I still love.

Some I will love forever.

I hope.

My track record isn't great with forever.

Or never.

So, I check my records.

Snowfall.

My first ever.

I wish that I could tell you I remembered.

"Lost"

When I reached the bottom of the bottle and wasn't numb,

I knew that it was over.

With you.

With me.

With my vice.

The world burned,

And I was forced to become my own community.

An impossible task made even harder from the scars.

I survived the fire.

It changed me.

My mind.

My body.

I feel empty...

And lost...

"Quail Ridge: Part 1"

I make a left at Lassiter Mill.

I've been here many times before.

The bookstore.

I remember 29.

January.

I met YOU...

Well, kinda...

We'd already met online.

You were instantly my favorite.

We paid too much for coffee and sandwiches.

Then, we found ourselves here.

It was raining.

And I was so happy.

Lassiter Mill became my favorite road

Because it reminded me of my favorite person.

I barely remember 30.

But I remember the drive.

The air.

The lights.

31.

I'm seated outside of the bookstore.

It's as beautiful as ever. And I just cry.

"Mid-Spring"

Season 4 of the hardest year.

Today, I had a panic attack.

Unprovoked.

Worry creeps in.

I know that the next season will not be any easier.

It is hard to stay present when the past haunts you,

And the future frightens you.

Inhale.

Exhale.

I am here.

I am breathing.

I am supported.

I am protected.

And despite the fear.

The depression.

The anxiety.

I am happy to be here.

And I am prepared.

"Dishes: Part 1"

Water and bubbles in the big pan.

The air smells of coffee and Dawn.

Cinnamon rolls are in the oven.

The calm before the store.

Inhale.

Exhale.

It's time to worry less about what the others will say.

Inhale.

Exhale.

I'll be alright.

I'm prepared for the night.

The dusk.

The dawn.

And the day.

"Contempt"

Pejorative.

For a master of numbers, you have a way with words.

The mind games are silly.

I cackle as I descend into madness.

"Dishes: Part 2"

Last night, I dreamt of you.

You weren't anything like I remember.

You were so kind.

We laughed.

I washed your dishes.

I don't remember what we talked about.

I just remember how I felt.

At ease.

I awoke this morning to a harsh reality.

You're not like that.

Not really.

Not to me.

The truth turned the tables.

You are a dream in my subconscious mind

And an absolute nightmare when I am awake.

Inhale.

Exhale.

This feeling...

Of doom and despair...

It's a tough one to shake.

"Discard"

If I am being honest with you,

I think we have a common goal.

Because I wish you'd forget me too.

And I'm not sure how you plan to do that as long as you keep playing the poorly written movie starring me.

"Lyrics"

I don't know what to say.

I read your words,

And they were beautiful.

I was moved...

Here I am again...

Wishing you well.

How?

How can I wish you well after you wished me dead?

We haven't spoken in a month.

I have been busy...

Picking up the shattered pieces of me

With assistance from my loved ones

And tiny orange bottles.

The world has been turning,

And I am turning my life around.

Slowly.

But surely.

Healing takes time,

And I want to dance.

I know that I didn't forget how.

"False Allies"

I never cared about winning.

I only cared that I was safe.

That's what kills me.

I wanted to be seen.

I wanted to be heard.

And I wanted to be safe.

I could blame you for everything,

But I don't think that's fair to me to excuse the actions of "mutuals" who picked a side.

People who violated my privacy.

People who took advantage of my kindness as I rapidly descended into madness.

I wasn't safe.

They made sure of that.

So, I could apologize for all the crazy shit that I said when I was crazy...

But to be honest,

It wouldn't have gotten that bad had I felt safe.

And you know what?

I asked for safety.

And you ensured that I didn't get that.

So yeah. I don't blame you for everything.

But you are responsible for a lot of what happened.

And you wished me dead.

So, I can wish you well,

But that's a reflection of me.

Not of you.

"Narcissism"

It's strange to be both hated and mirrored.

I can't say that it doesn't hurt because it does.

It hurts to see those who will mirror you worship you for your words,

And I know the words that you spoke to me in private.

It makes me wonder... is this what it means to lead by example?

I feel jealous.

And jaded.

Because I'd like to think that the world is better because I suffered

And that people will learn the weight that their words carry.

But it just doesn't feel real.

I don't want to be a martyr for a false cause.

I want to speak.

I want to create.

I want to dance.

And I hope that one day, I am valued in the way that others value you when you mirror me.

But not exactly.

I do not wish to be worshipped.

I just wish to be treated respectfully.

"Thanking a Scientologist"

I'm back in the city.

My mind is a little clearer than it was a week ago.

Questions linger.

I thank the man who wrote to me a month later.

We don't believe in the same deity,

And it seems odd to extend my gratitude.

Everything about the situation is odd.

I will never understand how the last many months were hard on you.

Assuming you are telling the truth anyway.

It would hardly be your first lie.

I wonder if you can feel guilt.

Shame.

And all the feelings that I'm capable of feeling.

It's strange to argue with a person who has such a skewed image of self.

I know what led to my break.

And I know why I was so vulnerable to begin with.

It's FUCKED up, but I feel conflicted.

I know the right answer.

I MUST pick myself this time.

And I know what that means for me.

It just scares me.

I don't want to lose any more time,

And I don't want to lose my mind.

"Storage"

I'm seated a story in the air.

Moving 200 pounds of my old life out of storage

So that I can give myself another shot at this business.

If I could go back in time, you and I never would have met.

Or if we did, I would not have allowed you to become special to me.

I sacrificed my sanity in the name of inspiration.

My feet dangle above the gray.

Am I a better person than I was before?

A better artist?

I guess we'll find out.

"Dear John"

I draft up my letter...

And attach the message that I received...

When you disclosed your insecurities and addressed it to me.

And then I stop myself.

Dear John,

You may fight this war with yourself, but I no longer come to your defense in your battles.

Because the war you wage you say is with me.

But it isn't.

It's a war you fight within your mind.

Your body.

Your soul.

I cannot tend to your wounds because I haven't stopped picking the shrapnel from my own.

I bid you farewell, and I decide for myself that we are not to speak again.

Is it still goodbye if the letter is never sent?

"Counts"

Inhale.

It's April

And it finally feels like spring.

Exhale.

I just finished weeping between the four walls of my first love of the city.

It was the first time in a long time that my tears were not accompanied by a panic attack.

I slipped on my shoes and began my trek through the neighborhood that I once called solace.

And I still do.

The neighborhood has changed.

As have I.

We grow but we remain tethered.

I was never good at never.

And I'm still unsure if I am any good at forever.

Maybe I can learn to be good at now...

Inhale... 2. 3. 4. 5. 6. 7. 8.

Exhale... 2. 3. 4. 5. 6. 7. 8.

"Uninvited"

Learn how to behave.

I know that seems laughable coming from me.

But baby, mental health episodes don't last forever.

Mine sure didn't.

So why are you, a stranger, still lurking?

Consider your role in the lives of the people that you lurk on and lurk for.

If you are no one to either of us, what exactly are you doing here?

"Breath"

I stopped holding my breath for the approval of others...

When I realized that they dream of a world where I choose to stop breathing.

I have decided...

That won't be an option for me.

"Consultation"

One call.

That's all it took to send me home in tears.

One call that made me feel like I wouldn't be believed.

That I would forever be the villain.

That the heartache and harassment would never stop.

Helpless.

I feel helpless.

It's exhausting to stick up for myself.

Is it not enough that I suffered?

I guess not...

The way of the world is corrupt and unkind.

And I don't know what kind of reaction to that is considered appropriate.

"Emote"

You taught me how to express emotions.

I never thought that you'd use those emotions against me.

I'm not acting a part when I move.

Sadness.

I consider my options to protect myself.

My reputation.

My privacy.

My future.

I do not take a decision like this lightly.

I do my research.

I learn of the impact that each option could have on your life.

And I grieve.

Because you put me through Hell.

And you haven't stopped.

I wonder if there will come a time that you lay down your weapons.

That you apologize.

I don't know why I continue to have faith in your ability to change.

Believe people when they show you who they are.

I showed myself to be a fool.

"Time Machine"

If I could go back in time, I wouldn't have stood up for myself publicly...

And disclosed to you privately that I was afraid of you...

If I knew then what I know now, I would have accepted your actions as goodbye,

And I wouldn't have praised the company that you keep.

I would have come to terms with their silence,

And I would have accepted that as goodbye too.

I wasn't crazy then...

But I was stressed.

Because I was going through a major life change.

And then came you.

You spoke the words into the world like a Prophet.

You told people that I was a mad woman...

Over, and over, and OVER again...

Until I finally was.

If I could go back in time, I would have faced my fears.

I would have attended the show.

I would have shown off my creations.

I would have made new connections.

And if you approached me, I would have greeted you with a smile.

A mask.

To cover my fear,

My frustration,

And my anger...

With you...

And your ignorance.

I would have said hello and goodbye.

And I would have meant my goodbye.

If I could go back in time, I would have risked the panic attack.

I would have faced you.

Because I was vulnerable then,

But I'm a lot more vulnerable now.

And unfortunately...

I cannot go back in time.

"Mask"

Had I known then what I know now,

I would have FUCKING FAKED IT.

"Dialogue"

I've written out the question, but I cannot bring myself to hit send.

I know it was you in the end.

But was it you all along?

And if it was, are you really that afraid to confess?

Are you really that afraid to take responsibility?

Because if it wasn't you, then you know who it was.

So why play along?

Is your ego so fragile that you would rather I sacrifice my life than live to learn the truth?

If we are standing at our podiums in the Cathedral of Palms,

You and I are just supporting actors.

We are neither the protagonist nor the antagonist.

They are.

Because they know the lines,

And they deliver them with the deepest conviction.

The director calls the shots.

She doesn't prefer to hear from us.

Because we sort of know the lines,

But we have to improvise.

She does not care for improv.

The lines are to be read exactly as written.

We wait for our moment in the spotlight.

Me on stage left.

You on stage right.

And when it's finally our turn, they cut our scene early.

We don't get to finish the dialogue.

I'm sure you have dreamed of the scene.

Over, and over again.

I learned a few lines last season.

Different cast.

Different director.

Different audience.

For an entertainer, you think that I could tolerate the theatrics.

But I sit here... hoping... praying... that my role is recast.

"Limerence"

There's a fine line between love and hate,

But what if it was never love?

I look up limerence and compare it to love.

To my dismay, the signs point to love.

Overwhelmingly so.

Is it possible that limerence is the line I walk between love and hate?

I walk the line, but the rope is slacked.

I find myself swinging - emotion to emotion.

Unsure of how I am keeping my balance.

I decide to jump.

Hate.

I'm picking hate.

It's the most rational option.

I bend my knees and prepare to launch,

And in this moment, I am frozen.

My feet are still connected to the line.

I picked.

I committed to the leap.

It makes the most sense.

So, why can't I move?

"Linger"

I wish that my gratitude outweighed my sadness and anger that accompanies my trauma.

I learned how to make this beautiful thing.

And it looks silly, but... damn... was it hard.

I struggle with self-image.

I'm not good enough.

No one cares.

And then I see what I created on the sole of someone who no longer calls me a friend,

And I just think...

Damn...

I made that.

ME.

I don't think that there is a scenario that I would consider justice for my suffering.

Questions linger, and I will get my answers.

I always do.

But I'm afraid.

And the other half I save.

Because I'm not safe yet to speak my truth.

So, I save it for another day.

I cross my fingers and pray to a God that I don't believe in

That there will come a day that I can speak honestly. And unapologetically.

"Find Me"

And fuck me.

I want you to spit your words of vitriol between my legs.

I want to scream your name so loudly that the high forever scars your mind.

I want to leave your ears ringing.

I want it to ruin your life.

I want it to haunt you.

I want you to return to your lover...

I want you to think of me... thrashing in your mouth.

I want you to hate fuck him while you think of me.

"Forgiveness"

What if I remember who the FUCK I was before my self-esteem tanked?

What if I remember my education?

My work experience...?

And I integrate my life experience?

What if I'm not a bad girl?

What if I'm a good girl?

If I'm firm?

If I have boundaries?

If I stand on business?

Then what?

Because I'm done.

I'm done with petty shit.

I'm done with mind games.

I'm done with avoidance.

You can be fake with your allies,

But I will not allow you to be fake with me.

So, understand this.

I approach any situation with compassion.

WAY more than you are due.

Because that's who I am as a person.

I'm not vindictive.

And frankly, I will give you one million chances to make it right.

...so long as you REALLY make it right.

So, I remember who I am.

I shoot my shot.

I tell my truth.

I use my experience.

And if you are wise...

If you are compassionate...

I will give you the time of day.

Because I am willing to give you grace that you do not deserve

So that I can move on.

"Sweet Auburn"

Inhale.

The scent of smoke fills my lungs.

I have been coming here for a decade.

I can't believe it.

It looks exactly as it did in 2014.

I brought my husband here.

My mom here.

And I came here alone.

Countless times.

Through happy times.

Musical festivals.

Plays.

Weekend breathers.

And sad times.

Covid. For pickup.

I live here now.

And I'm a creature of habit.

I'll have the taco plate.

And then I will go home.

I will sleep.

Same building.

Different bed.

"Monsters"

I crawled into bed a few hours ago,

But I couldn't sleep.

I didn't weep today, but I felt like I needed to.

The whole day.

My jaw aches.

It has for months now.

I gaze out my window into the darkness.

The wind rages and darker than the night sky are the shadows of the trees flowing through the earth's breath.

It's terrifying.

And I can't look away.

The storm approaches, and I know what that means for me.

Another day indoors

Struggling with my darkest emotions and the physical pain that accompanies my thoughts of despair.

Tomorrow won't be easy.

Hell, I don't remember the last time I had a day that WAS easy.

I find myself protesting my need for sleep.

Because I know that tomorrow I will wake up to another day of agony.

Waiting to get better.

Trapped in my mind.

Trapped in a body that I don't have the energy to bathe.

With unbrushed teeth that have rapidly shifted these last few months.

I don't look away from the shadows outside.

I feel connected to them.

In the dead of the night, they look like monsters.

As do I.

"Depression: Part 2"

Another day of silent screams following a sleepless night.

I made myself shower and brush my teeth at 4AM

Desperate to fall into a slumber.

I shut my eyes, and when they opened, I was lying in a pool of sweat.

The day was already half over.

It shouldn't be this hard to be understood.

Or at the bare minimum, left to exist peacefully.

8 months.

My privacy has been violated for 8 months and counting.

It didn't seem like that big of a deal to me when I couldn't accept the truth.

When I could fabricate a story to justify its existence.

But now I'm back where I was 8 months ago.

It's there.

It hurts me.

And I'm not sure why I am expected to ignore it.

"Piedmont"

The rain came but faded quickly.

I decided not to go home.

Here I am.

Seated.

By the creek in the heart of the city.

I hear sirens in the distance, but they do not phase me.

Below me lies an abundance of blooms.

Yellow.

Right where the water pools.

I think back to 5... maybe 6 years ago?

In this place.

By the courts.

I listened to the band in the wind ask Angie to come back to bed.

And I found peace.

It's strange to be here now.

Seated.

Listening to the water trickle down stones and into the valley of green and yellow.

My thoughts race, but my body is still.

Back then, I thought that life would only get better.

Richer.

Fuller.

With love.

With music.

With moonlight dances.

With moments like then.

I'm seated by the creek, and my environment feels uneasy.

Had you told me then what I would feel now,

I would have stayed in the park until morning.

And absorbed every remaining second of that peace.

"Worry"

I worry most days that I will never heal...

Because most days, I think that the only cure to my illness is an apology.

It's an irrational thought.

Because the damage warrants far more than a simple apology,

And I know that the simple apology isn't coming.

My heart and my brain seem to be tied much tighter than I thought.

...than I hoped.

...than I'd like.

They seem to agree.

It's the bare minimum,

But it's all that they want.

I wish they wanted more.

"Settle"

What if I'm firm, but I'm soft?

What if I'm direct?

What if I ask for the bare minimum even though I deserve more?

It's better than asking for nothing.

What if I give you one last chance to make it right, and you finally do?

I keep my hopes high and my expectations low.

I do my part so that I can move on and stop asking what if.

Your name, your face, and your art will never grace my page again.

Can you say the same?

"Mirage"

I cannot believe my eyes.

I prepare to make my 3-mile trek into midtown to immerse myself in dogwoods when I see it.

It's over.

I consider writing you one last time, but I don't.

I remember how I felt the first time that I thought it was over...
and then it wasn't.

My body feels like it could crumble in this moment.

Inhale.

Exhale.

It is time to move on.

"Rose Goggles"

The air is warm.

I close my eyes, and all I see is rose.

My mind wanders, and this time, I let it.

There is no Hell to escape today.

My legs are heavy.

My skin is hot at the touch.

Imagination takes over, and I experience pleasure...

Unburdened by sadness and hatred.

No red.

No green.

No orange.

No Blue.

Only rose.

It's surreal.

I dream of days that I feel joy.

Comfort.

Today is my first.

I open my eyes and gaze forward into the atmosphere of rose and lilac.

I don't see them in my peripheral vision...

The ghosts...

The monsters...

They're not here.

I'm alone.

I lie in the grass,

And soak in the heat of the evening.

The earth below me is firm,

And I am still soft.

"Highs and Lows"

Yesterday was euphoric.

But today is not.

I no longer hold the hatred in my heart that I wanted so badly to claim.

It made the most sense.

But it wasn't true.

One gesture of compassion.

That's all it took for me to be honest with myself.

I wish us both peace.

I haven't found the peace I desire yet.

I'm back to ruminating on the past and worrying about the future.

But not in the ways that I did before.

This chapter is closed.

"Reality"

An error was made.

There was no mercy.

No compassion.

No gesture to make it right.

Just the same tales from unreliable storytellers.

I ponder the life that I planned for myself when I believed the good news.

And I decided that nothing has to change.

I am here.

I am alive.

I'm walking.

I'm creating.

I'm taking my time to heal,

To eat,

To shower,

To brush my teeth,

And I am preparing for a better future.

I am moving on,

I will not allow those who cannot... determine my fate for me.

This is my promise to myself.

There may never be justice.

I may never know peace.

But I will learn to walk with my demons, and I will move forward.

"Birthdays"

Day fades into night.

I observe the sky's gradient.

Blue-gray to cream.

Soon, a blanket of indigo will cover the atmosphere.

I gaze through the trees and look within.

Why do I feel this way?

The movies play in my mind.

Birthdays.

The nights we felt alive.

The nights we danced.

Drinks.

Secrets.

Making meals and washing dishes.

The night we didn't think we would make it out of the bar...

I wonder how we could have shared these big moments,

But we will never speak again.

It's for the best, but it still aches.

Like the day, my friendships faded to darkness.

Indigo unfolds.

I lie below its cover...

Alone.

"Religion"

I wish that I believed in a God...

So that I could believe that you would face a Judgment Day.

If not in this lifetime.

Because believe you me.

If given the opportunity, I do not intend to be polite,

And I do not intend to be avoidant.

I intend to ask you directly...

To look me in the eye

Which is saying a lot because I'm Autistic,

And tell me why you did it.

Or why you didn't.

Because I do not care if it brings you shame.

It should.

You caused me suffering,

And I deserve answers.

"Venom"

Maybe I don't wish you well.

Because I'm not doing well.

My brain hurts so badly from wondering day in and day out what it's going to take to get my name out of your FUCKING mouth.

Maybe I don't hate you.

But I sure as Hell don't love you.

I keep telling myself that I will find peace if I just ignore it.

Be the bigger person.

No.

I can't find peace because you're still SCREAMING...

About the big bad crazy BITCH who suffered at the hands of you and your flying monkeys.

You are no Devil, and you are no God.

Just a sorry ass human who created a beautiful mask.

"The Movie"

I'll never be able to move on as long as it's live,

And I would like to move on.

The words I wrote her.

A truth that I don't want to accept.

Many times, over, I begged for the bare minimum.

An honest conversation.

Basic human decency.

Protection.

Compassion.

She turned her nose up at me,

She called me a psycho.

She said I was unworthy of her pity.

And she kicked me while I was down.

Over, and over, and over again.

On Christmas.

On my birthday.

On hundreds of unholy days.

And on the days that I was most vulnerable.

If there was ever a question about why I fell into psychosis, I can tell you why.

Because of her.

Because of them.

And because of every twisted individual who volunteered to do their dirty work.

She may be a natural born creator, but her true calling lies in destruction.

There are no number of persons who praise her for "helping their mental health" that could equate to a direct apology to me.

Because MY mental health...

She DESTROYED it.

And she laughed while she did it.

"Woodlands"

I found privacy in the garden...

And let loose.

"Triggered: Part 2"

Another day escapes me.

Or did I escape another day?

I have boxes stacked high...

And all the supplies.

Who'd have thunk it?

That I'd be afraid to handle acrylic in my hands.

It reminds me of who I thought I'd be by now,

And I'm not sure if that's still what I want.

Maybe it's been so long that I just forgot?

Maybe I've unlearned every trick in my book.

It's scribbled down.

I'm pretty sure I know where.

Maybe I just don't want to look.

"Imposter"

It's so strange to me that you spent 17 days pretending to be me...

Yeah. You.

You live this sparkly life full of success...

So why me?

Did you intend to cause me further suffering while you were pretending?

Or were you screaming on your behalf...

Using me as your mask?

"Imposter"

"Revamp: Part 2"

In process, and so am I.

I practically drowned in my own sweat last night.

It's hard work climbing a mountain during an avalanche.

Two steps forward before the masses drop...

Pushing me miles back.

It's a miracle that I survived,

And that I still want to climb.

"Cake"

I wonder if I will be wishing a 1st birthday to my biography born of bloodshed.

Will the Prophet throw a party to celebrate her predictions fulfilled of the woman gone mad?

Who will attend?

Oh, right. Them.

The fandom built on a fantasy so nefarious,

You'd think we'd fucked...

Will there be cake? And what name will be on it if so?

Who will blow out the candles if not me?

Will the partygoers play games to compete for the honor?

Will tiny claws be swept swiftly through the frosting and licked from their fingers while no one is looking?

Will the night end while it is still fun,

Or will it slowly die with disgrace?

"Rage"

I marched to the beltline just to lie down and look at the sky.

The days get closer, and I feel myself sinking into the pit of despair.

Of rage.

Because I have words for you.

And you're too much of a coward to let me say them to your face.

I don't want the world to see that side of me.

Because they already labeled me as a mad woman.

You're mad like me, and you know it.

And I'm suffering in ways that I cannot disclose...

So, I became a poet.

"The Lake"

I went to the lake to change the scenery for my weeping eyes.

Passion lost.

A truth that I can only tell if I water it down,

But it would still be too bitter for the public.

Is it my mind specifically?

Or are these big emotions a normal reaction to what I've experienced?

One hour of a past tale told with 2.5 to go.

My fingers aren't in my ears this time,

And it makes me long for the time that they were.

I was not ready to accept the truth in the winter.

I didn't believe you to be so frigid.

It's April. Almost May. And cold like it was in the fall.

My palms are burning.

And the rest of me...

I feel like I'm freezing again.

Is it my hypervigilance or my intuition?

I don't know.

My mind and body are just telling me that I need to survive.

"Intuition"

I sense that you are leaving the door cracked.

Once again, I'm unsure if that's my intuition or a delusion.

I don't spend my time waiting on your return.

But I spend a lot of time wondering who to hate the most.

Who to blame the most.

And I can tell you this...

I'm not busting through doors uninvited.

But I keep my door cracked too.

"Jealousy"

If I HAVE to be honest with myself?

God, I hate that.

I'm always going to be upset.

And jealous.

Because you picked them over me.

And that just makes me feel so insecure.

How could I value the approval of someone who doesn't value me?

It makes me feel so little.

"Triggered: Part 3"

My nerves are firing again.

I reach towards the handle,

And I shut the door.

I want so badly to be right.

But GODDAMNIT, I bled enough.

I'm not strong enough to carry the burden of sorrows from my foes.

They kicked me while I was down.

It's time to stop justifying to myself their actions.

They need no help in that matter.

Toxic.

Everything was toxic.

And it still is.

"Diagnosis"

I'm worried.

For me.

For so long, I have been fighting just to stay alive.

I see my debt accrue and my cash deplete.

Personally.

Professionally.

I was thinking last night... I feel like I missed two years of training.

I moved.

I got a shoulder injury.

I started a business.

My world fell apart.

I moved again.

And then I moved one more time.

I spoke out against my abuser, and then I took it down.

Over, and over again.

I always returned to her.

To protect her.

But she never protected me.

I will never understand how a failure lives rent-free in the head of such a star.

Except I do.

Time and time again, I watch the patterns.

And I know.

Sometimes, I feel jealous.

She spends so much time hurting me.

My reputation.

My mind.

My ability to make money.

And still runs two businesses.

I wish that I was that big of a powerhouse.

I'm not sure that I ever will be.

I'm still trying to survive.

Most days, I get out of bed.

That's a huge improvement for me.

But I worry.

Time feels limited.

Funds certainly are.

And I worry because I don't see a future for myself.

10%.

20 years.

The diagnosis...

I know now.

People like me...

10% of them take their own lives.

On average, they die 20 years before their counterparts without borderline.

I saved because I hoped to retire.

Retirement now keeps me alive.

Housed.

Fed.

And I'm worried.

I've never not been able to picture my future.

"Triggered: Part 4"

It happened.

The panic attack that made my teeth chatter so badly that it hurt.

And the words just escaped me.

Not for reasons that you'd think.

All those insecurities come flooding back.

Always too much.

Or never enough.

The words said about me that I knew were never true.

Dangerous.

Untreated.

Unmanaged.

Unhinged.

And the words that have been true for a long time.

Impulsive.

Emotional.

Alone.

"Dread"

There are many things that I wish on my worst enemy.

A bad haircut.

Acne.

A bad Google review written by anyone other than me.

But this feeling.

This destitute hole of darkness with edges so slick that one tremble in the earth launches me headfirst into the abyss...

Lined with ledges that are both sharp and fragile.

With caverns where the monsters hide and await my descent.

I fell again. I hit a ledge.

And I don't want to rest to start climbing back to the surface.

THAT FEELING.

I don't wish that on my worst enemy.

"Ideations"

My life doesn't feel like it's worth living today, and that is just too bad.

I have lost count of the days in the last year that I felt this low.

Oftentimes before or after a traumatic event.

Sometimes, it's my anxiety.

Oftentimes, it's my intuition.

Telling me that it's time to kick my body into survival mode.

I have survived many days like this one.

I will survive today.

I will survive the rest of the days this week.

Even if I am greatly disappointed.

And I already am.

Disappointed.

Again.

"Dismissal"

You'd think I'd be outraged.

With them.

With the system.

With myself.

But honestly...

I became numb to it all a long time ago.

And I am just... relieved...

Relieved to never sit in the Cathedral of Oaks

With a pounding heart

Chattering teeth

And rivers of tears.

Relieved to never scream at the sight of them.

Or gasp at the words that slip from their tongues.

Or demand to be heard by the men who interrupt me...

Who laugh at me...

I am relieved.

Because I grew tired of studying them.

Overanalyzing them for any ounce of humanity.

Compassion.

ANYTHING to indicate that maybe I was wrong.

Or understand them.

So, I'm not outraged.

I'm just relieved.

Inhale.

Exhale.

I never have to breathe the same air as them again.

"Grudge"

Outrage.

I didn't feel it earlier because I understood.

And I knew... there was not an ending that would make me happy.

Just one that would make my life easier.

And two that would make my life harder.

I feel it now.

I start to respond, and then I stop.

I can't let anybody see me angry.

Not now.

I paid the price when I spewed my venom.

And it cost me my reputation.

Because suddenly...

I became the monster that the Prophet foretold.

It wasn't worth it.

My mind.

My money.

My time.

My body.

So, I'm angry now.

Anyone in my position would be.

But I pose the question...

I know why I am angry...

But you got what you wanted.

Every. Time.

All I got was traumatized...

And this stupid shirt.

So why are you angry with me?

"Home"

I want to come home.

I stopped fearing the people here maybe two months ago.

But the establishment...

And the establishments that I once considered safe for people like me...

Because I WAS safe when I was there.

I WAS happy when I was there.

It's making me feel like going to Atlanta did, in fact, save my life.

Let's say that you didn't do it...

Okay...

But then your allies did...

And I don't know who did what... EXACTLY.

But you...

All of you...

You told me when I was at my lowest that the world would be better off without me.

And then my lowest got even lower.

So, I propose the question again.

Why are you angry with me?

If it's about money, I guarantee you that I lost more.

And you ensured that.

I can understand saying you didn't do it.

But to say it didn't exist?

Baby, even I'M not THAT delusional.

I remember my complaint.

Not to the establishment.

But to them.

Boring.

They did this to me.

And they aren't even interesting.

At least if it was you... or her... or them... WHOEVER, I would be flattered.

Others would DIE for that kind of attention.

And it was you.

And them.

And others.

And as it turns out...

I'm only flattered when I'm masking.

But truly...

I am not flattered.

I'm just annoyed.

Because I still feel like nobody...

But I must be SOMEBODY.

"Fixated Person"

I remember when I told you that I wasn't in love with you.

Because I wasn't.

You were my favorite.

But my favorite means something different.

Idealized.

Untrue.

A version of yourself you'd like to be.

And I'd like you to be.

But you aren't.

I remember when I told you that I wasn't in love with you.

It was just a symptom of my mental illness.

It has a term, ya know?

Favorite person.

But some people call it a fixated person.

You were mine.

But the real you...

You fail to live up to my expectations...

I won't ever forget you.

But I don't love you.

And you're not my favorite.

I hope that you grow.

And I hope you live a long life.

FAR from me.

But I'm not waiting for you to profess your love.

And I'm not waiting for your apology.

Not after this.

You have a long way to go before you understand the nuance of the situation.

Ironic considering you called yourself the Queen of Nuance.

Sounded cool.

But it just... wasn't true.

Gray.

Everything is gray.

It's a shame you only think in black and white.

"Quail Ridge: Part 2"

I'm seated in a large, tufted chair.

Surrounded by books.

I paced the aisles, and then it started.

My heart began to race.

My teeth began to chatter.

And my body began to shake.

So, I took a seat.

My eyes are dry.

I already cried earlier.

I don't feel like a person.

I don't even feel like a monster.

I feel like a myth.

A ghost.

A brain.

An unreliable one.

Caged.

In a meat sack.

Seated.

At the bookstore.

I'm grieving.

Because I talked to my favorite actor.

He read me the lines.

And I knew...

The part written for me had been recast.

The words exit my brain...

And slip from my fingertips.

Suddenly...

I'm crying... again.

"Doubt"

What if you only feel like a person when you make art...

And now they are laughing at that too?

"Surrender"

What do you do when the war you have waged so long is finally over?

What do you do when you finally get what you want?

But in the process, you burned every bridge?

Every street?

Every house?

And every field?

What do you do when the war you waged leaves you broke?

Broken?

Burned?

Burnt out?

What do you do when the war is over... but the question that might kill you was never answered?

What do you do if the fear is finally gone... but not knowing... REALLY... not knowing... continues to fuel the war in your mind?

What do you do when you finally get your way... but you're pretty sure that it's only because you learned to play the game?

Not because of compassion.

Not because of empathy.

And DEFINITELY NOT in the interest of truth.

Or justice.

What do you do when the war is over,

But the games continue?

Maybe not with them...

But with the town that burned.

What then?

"Triggered: Part 5"

Frozen.

The air is hot, but I am frozen.

My thoughts are no longer consumed by what I will do.

They are consumed by what I can make of it all.

With the thoughts.

The emotions.

The stories.

The one-liners.

True or not.

Said aloud or said in private.

And can I put glitter on it?

"Proverb"

"All is fair in love and war."

I don't believe that.

But you do.

So, tell me... what's it for you?

Love?

Or war?

"Shame"

I fear that I will always be stupid.

And desperate.

Desperate to make it all stop.

And stupid enough to do just about anything to make it all stop.

I felt like I needed to keep an eye out.

For my safety.

And now... I think it's time that I detach.

Completely.

I cannot control what people say about me.

And it is time that I stop letting their words control me.

I am a person.

I deserve to be alive.

And maybe I'm still stupid.

Maybe I'm still desperate.

Maybe I'm still weird.

But what do I expect?

It's a miracle that I am still alive after the last year.

"Afterparty"

When the show was over,

I spoke with one of the actors.

We reviewed the lines.

The scenes.

The plot.

The characters.

I ran my fingers through my hair and sighed.

I do not want to be in this theatre again.

The show was too long.

And I didn't like how it ended.

"Performance Art"

I wonder if I'd been permitted to adequately grieve...

Through performance art

If things would have gone differently.

I wonder if I would have been spared...

From all of it.

"Hatred"

I hate you.

Because I used to love you dearly.

Your words of vitriol... I can publish them... no problem.

But the words you said in private...

For years...

I just can't... but I guess I can... I just wished that I still believed them.

I wonder if you ever fixate on the past.

The words said before... everything.

Did you mean them?

Any of them?

You say that you choose your words carefully...

So, what am I supposed to make of these?

I love you.

I'm excited for you.

This makes me laugh.

That was beautiful.

I could FEEL that you needed comfort.

I love your playfulness.

What am I supposed to do with these words?

From before a time that I hated you so deeply.

I hate you.

Because I used to love you.

I used to be happy for you.

I used to be excited for you.

I used to want to be like you.

I used to praise you for your accomplishments.

And now...

I regret finding my identity in you.

Because I just... don't believe you anymore.

And that FUCKS me up.

Worse than anything you did to me this last year.

I always believed you.

I always believed IN you.

And now... I hope you fail.

Like I did.

And I hope that we both rebuild.

And that one day, you'll say you're sorry.

I already did.

I could hate you for every casualty that stepped between twin flames fueled by big emotions...

But they made their choices.

You make yours.

And I make mine.

My flame is out.

All that remains is smoke of the person that I once was...

And I'm okay with being the smoke that drifts away.

A million particles of me scatter into the air.

And I hope it haunts you.

I haunt you.

Because what you did was unforgiveable.

But I'll never forget you.

Ever.

"Abandonment"

I wish that I could blame the moon.

Or blame my brain.

I wish that I could say that I was confused.

Or wrong.

I wish that I could say that an explanation is enough.

That it doesn't hurt me.

But it's not true.

I wish that I had the self-respect that I need to make it in this life.

I wish that I could flourish.

Not just worry about surviving.

I wish that I'd been 100% to blame.

Because then it would be easy to understand.

To forgive.

Of course! I was in the wrong!

I was nuts!

But fundamentally, I don't think that's it.

I think that my insanity became a by-product of my circumstances.

And I warned everyone.

From the closest of confidantes to the unsuspecting onlookers.

I'm vulnerable.

Don't test me.

On my best days,

I feel like a ghost in the place that I once called home.

And on the worst,

I feel like the ruler of my own Hell.

This time...

I don't think my big emotions are to blame.

I think that they are warranted.

I feel like a ghost in the place that I once called home.

"Excuses"

I think that I have been using my mental illness as a crutch.

But not in the way that people say that I do.

My mental illness is an explanation, not an excuse.

I talk about my mental illness because that's my reality.

That's my warning to the world.

I'm vulnerable.

Don't test me.

I think that I use my mental illness as a crutch...

But not to excuse my own behavior.

To excuse yours.

Because it is hard for me to come to terms with my reality.

I was victimized.

I was exploited.

I became weak.

I was hurt.

And I take accountability for the ways in which I fucked up.

Because I understand that there are consequences for my actions.

So sometimes it's easier for me to blame it all on my mental illness.

"I was crazy."

"It was understandable."

"They were justified."

But they weren't.

We're not the same.

I have cognitive empathy for those whose experiences differ from mine.

I have emotional empathy for those who do not reciprocate my level of emotional empathy.

I'm often driven by emotions blended with logic.

I use my mental illness as a crutch...

A support...

Because I cannot come to terms with piss poor behavior

Of those who preyed on my mental illness...

And I cannot come to terms...

With the real feelings of loneliness that led to the delusions.

"Dissociation"

If I could undo the last year... would I?

Realistically... no.

Because I think I'm actually going to get better.

And my reality is... I can't undo the last year.

My brain and body will carry those scars with me for the remainder of my days.

Right now

I'm taking reprieve...

In this level of dissociation that allows me to look at every experience from the last year...

And think about it in stories.

As if it happened to someone else.

And I'm just an onlooker.

I was thinking about this the other night and wrote about it.

I burned bridges.

And I would burn them all over again.

The way that people chose to interact with me was not acceptable.

I get a bit of FOMO watching others have fun within social circles.

But past that...

I dare not allow those who did not care about me...

Say that they did...

And that they were "just trying to help".

Especially strangers.

I have deep control-based childhood wounds.

I'm the age my dad was when I was born.

But I still feel infantilized.

People aren't happy with me unless they can control me.

And I'm just not down with that.

"Service"

I'm ready to be done.

Because this connection isn't worth my life.

Obsessed.

You became obsessed with me.

And I don't know what to make of it.

Am I a star?

Am I flattered?

Or am I just done?

Because you became obsessed with my failure.

You became obsessed with interference.

You let others fight the battles that you were too weak to fight yourself.

In fact, you made up a war that just... DIDN'T fucking exist...

You torched my world for your entertainment.

You lied.

And lied.

And lied.

You never wanted me to get better.

And right here.

Right now.

I know.

I'm going to get better.

I'm going to write.

I'm going to draw.

I have plans to make my life better.

But I MUST face you first.

You started this.

I'm ending it.

I'll see you when I see you.

And then I pray that I never see you again.

"For Old Time's Sake"

Hey. It's me.

The city looks beautiful tonight.

I thought about writing you for old time's sake,

But I didn't.

The humid air in my lungs and the heat of 100 degrees brought me a joy I have long forgotten.

Maybe I'll stay.

Go to the beach.

Visit Mickey.

Idk.

But for the first time in a long time,

I think I'm right where I need to be.

I'll see ya in the Cathedral of Palms.

And after that...

Idk.

Maybe never.

But whatever happens, I'm reminded of something that I lost in the City of Oaks.

I want to live a beautiful life.

A long one.

"Anticipation"

I've felt this feeling many times before.

Palms tingling.

Alone.

But things are different this time.

I'm confident.

I'm prepared.

For the best.

And for the worst.

I open my pill bottle.

Place one in my mouth.

Swallow it down.

And pop a strip of gum in my mouth.

I'll be okay.

I am worthy.

I am loved.

I am going to be okay.

"LOSS"

The worst happened.

So, what do I do now?

Maybe go to the beach.

Or go home.

Connect with those who care about me.

Those who love me.

Write.

Poetry.

Stories.

Fiction maybe.

Don't vomit on the floor.

Or do.

I was disgraced before I became bold.

"Extended Stay"

I'm glad I stayed.

I worked hard.

Printed everything.

I wrote. And wrote. And wrote.

Nearly 7000 words.

Because, for the first time in a long time,

I feel okay enough to fight.

Not fawn.

Not fly.

Not freeze.

Fight.

Because my rights are at stake.

My reputation is at stake.

And I'm the only one who walked away from the last year with PTSD.

And a psychotic episode.

I said what I needed to say.

In case I can't say anything else for a long time.

But I have options.

This time, I'm fighting for me.

And if I don't get my way...

Fine.

But I have more pride in myself if I fight for myself...

...than if I lie down and concede to the abuse.

I'm not a doormat.

I am not the words of vitriol that have been spewed at me.

But I am strong AF.

Even when I'm fragile.

For the first time in a long time, I'm confident.

I'm doing my part.

And even if I don't get my way,

It was worth my time to fight for me.

"Motion"

10 hours of driving

In under 48 hours.

6 hours waiting.

Less than an hour to say my piece.

A panic attack...

...so disabling that my legs gave out after I screamed my final words.

Hours upon hours organizing and reformatting.

235 pages when it was too late.

12 hours writing.

7000 words.

16 exhibits.

A choice.

To fight for my reputation.

To fight for a better life for me.

Because it happened to me.

I got PTSD.

I had a psychotic episode.

I was smeared.

I was provoked.

I was disrespected.

My husband was disrespected.

My mother was disrespected.

So, I'm putting up a fight.

Because I'm not all the words said about me.

I am not the rivers of vitriol spewed upon my name.

I am strong.

I am loved.

I am worthy.

Even if I carry the burden of this disgraced title.

And one thing is for DAMN sure...

I'm not a failure.

"Sick"

I am so sick of fighting.

I am so sick of crying.

I am so sick of being ridiculed for every embarrassing thing that I did when my mind was so sick.

Because I'm embarrassed.

I truly am.

I'm sick of apologizing.

I'm sick of trying to make peace.

This is my promise to myself.

I want to heal.

And if you have not experienced what I did... then you really do not know what it is like.

Disengage.

I'm done.

I'm Cissy.

I make glitter heels.

I draw.

I write.

Sometimes I tell jokes.

Sometimes I overshare.

I'm more than my past,

And I deserve a better future.

No matter what happens.

No matter what is said about me.

I am not linear.

I am a force of vibrant colors and the deepest darkness.

"Guilty"

I was guilty. Per the queen. Off with her head!

And I argued with her.

It was never malicious.

And I couldn't explain it...

But it wasn't willful.

It was compulsive.

So many Batshit things said while at rock bottom.

And I screamed...

IF IT HAPPENED TO YOU, WHY WOULDN'T YOU STICK UP FOR ME?

And the queen said to me...

The town had no obligation to you. Off with her head!

And my head rolled.

The words I said were malicious...

But the words said to me were "not nice".

The words said to me about being dead to the town... as I developed SI.

I was so angry with them. Still am.

But honestly... these systems...

This hierarchy.

If you are making decisions that will affect a person's life based on what happened on social media...

But you don't GET social media... as I learned that many royals don't...

Don't you think it's time that you learn?

Before you make a life-changing decision?

She told me that my mental illness isn't an excuse. I know.

I've heard it.

Over and over and over.

But it's an explanation that the townspeople and the royals blow off.

Because the truth about me doesn't fit their narrative.

It isn't scary enough.

It isn't entertaining enough.

And they can't be a hero if it is true.

Every. Single. One. Of. Them.

It's me. Hi.

I'm the monster on the hill.

"Testimony"

I found peace in two lies.

They were soft.

One.

Two.

Like when a musician counts down before playing one of their greatest hits... Stripped down... during a private acoustic set.

The frogs sing tonight,

I am at ease...

1... 2.... . . . .

I imagine my fingers plucking at brass strings while I gaze out to an audience.

Thank you for joining me tonight.

I wrote this song about a decade ago.

I retreated to the city to find myself during my first psychotic episode...

And it saved my life.

"Manifesto"

Part of me hopes that my manifesto is set ablaze.

Because I don't want to return.

Not even to fight for what I asked.

I bear this wound in my side.

The kind that grows inflamed and just never quite closes.

A reminder of what happened.

I had this hope that being polite would be enough for my flesh to regenerate...

Or smart

Or interesting

Or kind

Or understanding

Every time I leave this city, I feel claws grab at my side...

Inflicting deeper lacerations.

I'm not sure how I haven't bled out by now.

I'm sick of preparing for the sermon.

I'm sick of reading scripture.

If I just surrender to the Devil, will it all be over?

I prepared my manifesto because I HAD to.

I'd never forgive myself if I didn't.

But truthfully,

I hope it burns.

"Tik... Tok..."

I don't know what to do.

How do I stand up for myself adequately?

I want to move on.

I gaze at the clock.

Tick... tock... tick... tock...

My window of opportunity is rapidly closing...

Do I stand up for myself from rock bottom?

Or do I let the window close?

In hopes that one day... I stop caring.

That the weight that sunk me to the ocean floor will finally come untethered from my ankle.

So that I can float to the surface.

It's a miracle that I'm still alive.

I've gone without oxygen for so long.

"Motion Denied"

...the manifesto was set afire.

Inhale.

Exhale.

I have always loved the scent of smoke.

"Last Fall"

I wrote this poem for me.

Because I lost my way.

My identity. Stripped.

My voice. Stripped.

My community. Stripped.

October 21, 2023.

The day that my stress level became so great...

That I began to suffer in a way I'd never experienced.

I wrote this poem under false pretenses.

To express gratitude.

But this...

This was always for me.

This is my art.

This is how I heal.

I create.

Because I'm an artist.

A poet.

A dancer.

And a creator.

"The Haunted House: Finale"

Have you ever seen such an unruly beast?

A body that thrashed so hard during an exorcism and survived?

I wasn't the first.

Others were infected.

But this I promise you...

I'm the last.

Because every palm that dared to penetrate my skin

To enter my mind and strip me of my humanity...

Burned.

They were never invited.

The souls of those who were once welcome became phantoms.

I regret allowing them to haunt me for so long.

The house that once stood tall like a Cathedral atop the greatest hill in town... it burned to the ground.

I lived.

I left.

And I will never return to its grounds.

Goodbye to The Haunted House.

You were grand...

But you were never safe.

"Revelations"

It's 3AM.

The sky is preparing to weep.

I already have.

I pick through my collection in search of commonalities.

And there they are.

I cannot believe my eyes.

What are the odds?

The phone is ringing.

Is that confirmation?

I stopped looking for signs after they led me astray.

I let it ring.

Two missed calls.

One caller.

(178)801-0570

They didn't leave a message.

But I know who.

I knew as they whispered...

One.

Two.

While I choked on the ash from a flame that once burned Blue.

"The Hotel"

I loved you when the floors were warped,

And the water ran brown.

I walk the labyrinth of this place.

Like I did for a decade.

We parted ways briefly.

She was Stripped.

Then restored.

I pick up my mail where I used to check in.

And be greeted by a black cat.

With a folded ear and full belly.

This place always felt like home.

"No Doubt"

I'M JUST A GIRL!

I scream as my nails grow into claws.

The hair on the back of my neck stands high to the Heavens.

I fall to my hands and knees to find that they have been replaced by giant paws of a creature of the night.

My amber eyes turn to black,

And before I know it, I'm howling.

The next morning, I wake.

Naked.

Afraid.

Alone.

What happened last night?

I can't remember.

"The Circus"

I fear that I may be trapped in this circus forever.

Always performing.

Whatever it takes to keep the audience smiling.

You'd think that they'd be entertained enough by the clowns.

But all eyes look up.

At me.

I feel a slack in the rope.

I lose my balance.

I fall and trust that I survive the impact.

Seems crazy, right?

The audience SHRIEKS.

They gather 'round and lean in to hear my words as they anticipate my last breath.

I keep them waiting...

Tik... tock... tik... tock...

To their dismay, I rise.

I walk out.

My lips are sealed.

"The Pool"

Seated.

At the edge of a pool.

With a heart half full.

And a mind overflowing.

A part of me misses the excitement.

The fight.

The mystery.

Everything.

Despite the pain.

The nightmares.

The feeling of dread.

I knew that I wanted to be done,

But I would have picked a different ending.

These days, I feel like I am riffing alone.

Online.

In a sea of viewers asking...

What's your damage?

"The Club"

Seated.

At a club.

With a social group.

For the first time.

In this city.

Ever.

Bombing.

Socially.

Because how do I come back from this?

A psychotic episode?

A fall from grace?

A social bond so volatile that it threatens my life after psychosis...

How do I let go?

Make new friends?

Relate?

Form bonds... at all?

What if I create art?

With my trauma?

And this time... no one is laughing?

What then?

People laughed while I suffered.

Can I make them laugh now?

Put on a show?

Sure.

But when the show is over...

Can I unmask?

Not drive this new community away...

Avoid my mistakes of yesteryear?

I don't want to get close.

My art feels like the only way out.

How do I network?

Socialize?

Make friends?

How do I do that when I have been alone for so long?

And is it even worth it?

"Closure"

Indifference.

To your well-being.

To your healing.

To your narrative.

I'm ready to confess my sins.

I wrote, and I wrote, and I wrote.

Beautiful words.

And iconic phrases.

Until you echoed them back to me.

My power. Stripped.

My voice. Stripped.

My community. Stripped.

My business. Stripped.

My soul. Stripped.

My brain. Stripped.

My body. Stripped.

It started as a spark.

In the season of Pisces.

The words fell from my lips.

I gazed into the audience.

At the Cathedral of Oaks.

The attendees were confused by my monologue.

And I grew uncertain.

My freedom. Stripped.

I breathed a sigh of relief as I was taken into custody.

Safe.

I'm finally safe.

I rested.

Truly rested.

For the first time.

Until my release...

Afterwards... I began seeding a garden.

On the grounds of The Haunted House.

Of insecurities.

Not mine.

Yours.

I watered them until they sprouted.

As the flame burned slowly,

I worked on myself.

Through my impulses.

And I kept watch.

Mirrored you...

I warned you in the summer...

I'm vulnerable.

Don't test me.

And then you did.

Over, and over, and over again.

Masked.

And unmasked.

Until I feared you.

And they feared me.

I lost my mind.

And began to love you.

Deeply.

And you felt powerful.

I don't think you meant it when you said it.

That you loved me.

But I did.

I wouldn't have hated you if I never loved you...

Machiavellianism.

Narcissism.

Psychopathy.

The Unholy Trinity that once laid dormant in me...

I know what I did to regain power.

After you took mine.

The Haunted House was set afire.

By me.

I nearly died.

As I inhaled the smoke.

Of a blaze burning bright and Blue.

They say that a narcissist will reveal herself.

I guess we always do.

...a suburban housewife.

That's who you are in my tale.

I'll tell my truth.

You can call me a liar.

And if your audience asks...

It's all fiction.

"It's better to be feared than to be loved."

I fear that may be true.

It's summer again...

How about that?

I pray that you fear me.

But I no longer fear you.

About the Author

Cissy Stag is an Atlanta-based writer, glitter heels maker, and stand-up comedian. She grew up in North Florida and has a Bachelor of Science in Risk Management & Insurance from Florida State University. Cissy is a member of the LGBTQIA+ community and is the proud owner of one maroon suit. She is a survivor of cyberstalking and stress-induced psychosis.